TEAM SPIRIT ®

SMART BOOKS FOR YOUNG FANS

THE NEW YORK JETS

BY
MARK STEWART

NORWOOD HOUSE PRESS

CHICAGO, ILLINOIS

Norwood House Press
P.O. Box 316598
Chicago, Illinois 60631

For information regarding Norwood House Press, please visit our website at:
www.norwoodhousepress.com or call 866-565-2900.

Editor: Mike Kennedy
Designer: Ron Jaffe
Project Management: Black Book Partners, LLC.
Special thanks to Topps, Inc.

Library of Congress Cataloging-in-Publication Data

Stewart, Mark, 1960-
  The New York Jets / by Mark Stewart.
     p. cm. -- (Team spirit)
  Includes bibliographical references and index.
  Summary: "Team Spirit Football edition featuring the New York Jets that
chronicles the history and accomplishments of the team. Includes access to
the Team Spirit website which provides additional information and
photos"--Provided by publisher.
   ISBN 978-1-59953-533-3 (library edition : alk. paper) -- ISBN
978-1-60357-475-4 (ebook)
 1. New York Jets (Football team)--History--Juvenile literature. I. Title.

 GV956.N37S74 2012
 796.332'64097471--dc23

                                                2012012312

Manufactured in the United States of America in North Mankato, Minnesota.
205N—082012

COVER PHOTO: The Jets celebrate a last-second win in 2011.

Table of Contents

ABOUT OUR GLOSSARY

In this book, there may be several words that you are reading for the first time. Some are sports words, some are new vocabulary words, and some are familiar words that are used in an unusual way. All of these words are defined on page 46. Throughout the book, sports words appear in **bold type**. Regular vocabulary words appear in ***bold italic type***.

Meet the Jets

Most football teams are remembered for their great players and thrilling games. The New York Jets have had plenty of both, but they will forever be linked to one amazing victory more than 40 years ago. On that day, in just the third **Super Bowl**, the Jets proved that a team with confidence and heart could accomplish anything.

Jets fans don't expect their team to win the Super Bowl every year. But they do demand that the players give a championship effort every time they take the field. Over the years, win or lose, this is what has made "Gang Green" a special team.

This book tells the story of the Jets. Their players have big dreams and big personalities. They have a way of making fans jump out of their seats and cheer as one. When you root for the Jets, you always need to be ready for takeoff!

Quarterback Mark Sanchez congratulates the defense on a job well done. The Jets make big plays on both sides of the ball.

Glory Days

The popularity that *professional* football enjoys today began in the 1950s. Back then, millions of fans began watching **National Football League (NFL)** games on television. In 1960, a group of businessmen decided there was room for a new league. The **American Football League (AFL)** was born. Most of the AFL

clubs began in cities where the NFL did not play. However, in New York City, a team called the Titans bravely took on the Giants, one of the best teams in all of football.

The Titans hired Sammy Baugh as their first coach. Baugh had been one of the NFL's most successful quarterbacks. Naturally, his teams loved to pass. The Titans had two great receivers in Don Maynard and Art Powell. They became the first teammates to each gain 1,000 receiving yards in the same season.

The Titans were fun to watch, but the Giants had far more fans and remained the most popular team in New York. It

took three of the smartest people in football to save the Titans. Leon Hess and Sonny Werblin bought the team and changed the name to Jets. They hired Weeb Ewbank to coach the team. Ewbank was well known to New York football fans. He had led the Baltimore Colts to the NFL championship twice—both times over the Giants!

Hess, Werblin, and Ewbank worked together to build a team around stars such as Joe Namath, Larry Grantham, Al Atkinson, Winston Hill, and Matt Snell. Namath was the most important player for the Jets. They signed him to the largest contract in football in order to keep him from joining the NFL's St. Louis Cardinals.

By 1968, the Jets were the top team in the AFL. Namath broke many of the league's passing records. He teamed with Maynard and a group of young stars to give New York a great offense. The defense, led by Grantham, was also very good. New York won the AFL championship and met Baltimore in Super Bowl III. The Jets shocked fans everywhere by beating the powerful Colts. The victory

LEFT: Art Powell   **ABOVE**: Joe Namath hands off to Matt Snell. They helped the Jets soar to a championship.

proved that the AFL was as good as the NFL. Two years later, the leagues *merged*.

Great things were expected of the Jets in the 1970s. New York had some terrific pass-catchers during this *era*, including Rich Caster and Jerome Barkum. But Namath suffered through one injury after another, and the team struggled.

By the early 1980s, a new group of players led Gang

Green. Joe Klecko, Marty Lyons, Abdul Salaam, and Mark Gastineau formed a great defensive line nicknamed the "New York Sack Exchange." Quarterback Richard Todd, running back Freeman McNeil, receiver Wesley Walker, and tight end Mickey Shuler paced the offense. McNeil eventually retired as New York's all-time leading rusher. In 1982, the Jets played for the championship of the **American Football Conference (AFC)** for the first time. Unfortunately, they lost to the Miami Dolphins.

LEFT: Freeman McNeil looks for daylight against the Chicago Bears.
ABOVE: Joe Klecko, Marty Lyons, Abdul Salaam, and Mark Gastineau were also known as the New York Sack Exchange.

New York fans grew hungrier and hungrier for another Super Bowl victory. But the Jets always came up short. In 1996, New York hired coach Bill Parcells to rebuild the team. He relied on four offensive stars—quarterback Vinny Testaverde, running back Curtis Martin, and receivers Keyshawn Johnson and Wayne Chrebet. Martin proved to be the best of this group. He wound up breaking nearly all of McNeil's records. The Jets made it back to the **AFC Championship Game** in 1998. But just as in 1982, the team fell one win short of a return trip to the Super Bowl.

The 21st century found a new group of stars in green and white. Quarterback Chad Pennington was surrounded by talented teammates, including Laveranues Coles, Santana Moss, Jerricho Cotchery, Leon Washington, and Thomas Jones. The team made it to the **playoffs** four times from 2001 to 2006, but it could not produce a championship.

The Jets eventually decided to make big changes. Rex Ryan was hired to coach the club. He made untested **rookie** Mark Sanchez his starting quarterback. Playing behind a line featuring Nick Mangold and D'Brickashaw Ferguson, Sanchez developed into a reliable leader who came up big late in games. Meanwhile, Bart Scott and Darrelle Revis led Ryan's defense. In 2009, the Jets won five of their last six games to make the playoffs. New York advanced to the AFC title game but lost to the Colts.

One year later, the Jets made the playoffs again. Sanchez had two new weapons, Santonio Holmes and LaDainian Tomlinson. They helped New York return to the conference championship game, but the Jets fell short again. In 2012, the Jets traded for quarterback Tim Tebow, hoping he could provide a winning edge. New York fans know it's only a matter of time before they celebrate another championship.

LEFT: Curtis Martin
ABOVE: Darrelle Revis

Home Turf

The Jets have called three stadiums home since 1960. They played their first four seasons in an old-time baseball stadium known as the Polo Grounds. From 1964 to 1983, the team played in Shea Stadium, which was also built for baseball. In 1984, the Jets moved to New Jersey. There, they hosted their games in Giants Stadium in the Meadowlands Sports Complex. They shared the stadium with the Giants. Both teams still called themselves "New York."

In 2010, the Jets opened a new stadium with the Giants. The Jets and their fans love the stadium because they no longer have to play on a field named after another team. On game days for the Jets, the stadium is decorated in green and white.

BY THE NUMBERS

- The Jets' stadium has 82,566 seats.
- It cost $1.6 billion to build the stadium.
- The stadium is one of the most environmentally friendly in the NFL. It was made with more than 60,000 tons of recycled steel, and seats were made from recycled plastic.

Jets fans get a great view of the field.

Dressed for Success

Football fans know the Jets for their green and white uniforms. But the original colors of the Titans were blue, gold, and white. The team used these colors until 1964. That season, new owner Leon Hess switched to today's familiar colors.

The Jets' uniform has stayed pretty much the same since the 1960s. The team changed to a darker shade of green in 1990, and sometimes New York wears its old colors for special games.

Over the years, the Jets have done a lot of experimenting with their helmet. In the 1960s, they wore a white helmet with green stripes and a green football with *JETS* written across it. In 1978, the team switched to green helmets and changed their **logo**. The new design showed a modern jet. In 1998, the Jets went back to a helmet that was closer to the original design.

LEFT: Bart Scott wears the classic green and white of the Jets.
ABOVE: Don Maynard poses in the blue and gold Titans uniform.

We Won!

The Jets are often at their best when they are **underdogs**. That was the case in Super Bowl III when they faced the mighty Baltimore Colts. No one expected New York to even keep the game close.

There was a lot on the line for pro football. Three years earlier, the AFL and NFL had decided to form one big league. The merger was scheduled to take place in 1970. Until the AFL and NFL joined forces, they agreed to face off each year in a championship game known as the Super Bowl. The NFL destroyed the AFL in the first two contests. That left many people wondering: What would happen

LEFT: Touchdown! Don Maynard tumbles into the end zone with the catch that sent New York to the Super Bowl.
RIGHT: Weeb Ewbank

if AFL teams could not compete with NFL teams?

As Super Bowl III neared in January of 1969, more and more people were asking that same question. The Colts looked unbeatable. They went 13–1 and also defeated the Cleveland Browns 34–0 for the NFL championship. It appeared that Baltimore would roll to another easy victory in the Super Bowl.

New York coach Weeb Ewbank had a different idea. Even though his team had far less experience than the Colts, he believed the Jets could beat them. New York had just defeated the Oakland Raiders for the AFL championship. Ewbank and his players were full of confidence.

No one was more confident than Joe Namath. He led an offense that had two good running backs—Matt Snell and Emerson Boozer—and a quick, smart offensive line. Namath also had several

Matt Snell

sure-handed receivers, including Don Maynard and George Sauer.

The Jets had a sensational defense as well. Larry Grantham called the plays for a unit that was ranked first in the AFL against the run and second against the pass. New York had the talent to shut down any offense.

Before the game, Namath guaranteed that the Jets would win. This angered the Colts. The experts had picked them to win by 19 points. By game time, the Baltimore players were losing their cool. Meanwhile, the Jets were calm and confident. Led by their fearless quarterback, New York played a great first half. The Jets used their quickness to gain an advantage over their stronger opponents. They also got a few lucky breaks. New York took a 7–0 lead into halftime. The Colts were in shock.

Nothing went right for Baltimore in the second half either. Namath barely had to throw the ball because of New York's great

rushing attack. Instead, he handed off to Snell, who kept picking up big yardage. The Jets controlled the pace of the game and padded their lead with three **field goals** by Jim Turner. The Colts scored a touchdown in the fourth quarter, but it was too little, too late. The Jets celebrated a 16–7 victory and their first Super Bowl championship.

As Namath ran off the field, he held up his index finger to show the world which team was the best. The real winner was pro football. No one would ever again doubt the decision to merge the AFL and NFL.

LEFT: Matt Snell led all runners with 121 yards in Super Bowl III.
ABOVE: Joe Namath lets the crowd know the Jets are #1.

Go-To Guys

T o be a true star in the NFL, you need more than fast feet and a big body. You have to be a "go-to guy"—someone the coach wants on the field at the end of a big game. Jets fans have had a lot to cheer about over the years, including these great stars …

THE PIONEERS

DON MAYNARD   Receiver

• BORN: 1/25/1935   • PLAYED FOR TEAM: 1960 TO 1972

Don Maynard was the first player signed by the Titans. The former college track star had 72 receptions in his first season with the team. By the time he retired, he had caught more passes for more yards than anyone in football history.

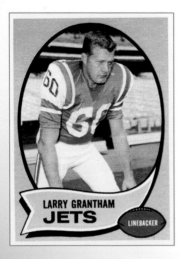

LARRY GRANTHAM   Linebacker

• BORN: 9/16/1938   • PLAYED FOR TEAM: 1960 TO 1972

During the 1960s, the Jets relied as much on their defense as they did on their offense. The heart of the defense was Larry Grantham. He played all 10 years that the AFL was in existence and was an **All-Star** five times.

WINSTON HILL   Offensive Lineman

BORN: 10/23/1941   PLAYED FOR TEAM: 1963 TO 1976

Matt Snell, Emerson Boozer, and John Riggins became stars running behind a group of blockers led by Winston Hill. He also did a great job protecting Joe Namath from pass-rushers. Hill set a team record by playing in 174 games in a row.

JOE NAMATH   Quarterback

• BORN: 5/31/1943   • PLAYED FOR TEAM: 1965 TO 1976

Joe Namath was the best passer in the AFL and then the NFL before knee injuries slowed him down. Namath was the **Most Valuable Player (MVP)** in Super Bowl III and the first pro quarterback to throw for more than 4,000 yards in a season.

JOE KLECKO   Defensive Lineman

• BORN: 10/15/1953   • PLAYED FOR TEAM: 1977 TO 1987

No one wanted to mess with Joe Klecko. He was a national boxing champion twice in college and one of the strongest players in the NFL.

MARK GASTINEAU   Defensive Lineman

• BORN: 11/20/1956   • PLAYED FOR TEAM: 1979 TO 1988

During the 1980s, the king of the **sack** was Mark Gastineau. He was almost impossible to block one-on-one. Gastineau was Defensive Player of the Year in 1982.

LEFT: Larry Grantham
RIGHT: Mark Gastineau

FREEMAN McNEIL   Running Back

- BORN: 4/22/1959   • PLAYED FOR TEAM: 1981 TO 1992

Few players in NFL history have been as hard to tackle as Freeman McNeil. He had size, speed, and great moves. McNeil led the NFL in rushing in 1982. Along with teammate Johnny Hector, he gave the Jets a great **backfield**.

WAYNE CHREBET   Receiver

- BORN: 8/14/1973

- PLAYED FOR TEAM: 1995 TO 2005

After graduating from college, Wayne Chrebet was not **drafted** by a single NFL team. He asked for a tryout with the Jets and soon became their top receiver. Chrebet was at his best on third down, when the team needed him the most.

CURTIS MARTIN   Running Back

- BORN: 5/1/1973

- PLAYED FOR TEAM: 1998 TO 2005

Curtis Martin was the best runner in team history. He gained 1,000 yards in each of his first seven seasons with the team and missed only one game. Martin was the NFL rushing champion in 2004 at the age of 31.

D'BRICKASHAW FERGUSON   Offensive Lineman

- BORN: 12/10/1983
- FIRST YEAR WITH TEAM: 2006

In 2006, the Jets rebuilt their offensive line around D'Brickashaw Ferguson. He was big, quick, and light on his feet. He also held a black belt in karate—which made him an even better blocker!

DARRELLE REVIS   Defensive Back

- BORN: 7/14/1985
- FIRST YEAR WITH TEAM: 2007

The Jets were thrilled to find Darrelle Revis still available when they made the 14th pick in the 2007 draft. After one season, opponents learned not to throw the ball his way. A couple of years later, many were calling Revis the best defensive player in all of football.

MARK SANCHEZ   Quarterback

- BORN: 11/11/1986   • FIRST YEAR WITH TEAM: 2009

The Jets made Mark Sanchez their starting quarterback as a rookie. He turned out to be a fast learner. Sanchez guided New York to the AFC Championship Game in 2009 and again in 2010. His greatest *asset* was his ability to remain calm under great pressure.

LEFT: Wayne Chrebet gets a hug after a touchdown.
ABOVE: D'Brickashaw Ferguson

Calling the Shots

Coaching a pro football team in New York is one of the best—and toughest—jobs in sports. Perhaps that is why the Jets have had so many *remarkable* people working on the sidelines. Their first two coaches—Sammy Baugh and Bulldog Turner—made the **Hall of Fame** as players. Weeb Ewbank was already an NFL legend when he arrived in New York. In the 1950s, he took over the young and disorganized Baltimore Colts. Under Ewbank, they became champions of the NFL.

With the Jets, Ewbank built a strong defense and added a powerful running game. His *reputation* as a great coach helped the team sign top players such as Matt Snell and Joe Namath, who might otherwise have joined NFL clubs. Ewbank taught the Jets to play hard and smart. They always took advantage when their opponents made a mistake. New York won the Super Bowl in Ewbank's sixth season.

The Jets came within one victory of returning to the Super Bowl four times in the years that followed. In 1982, their coach was Walt Michaels. He had played for Ewbank in the 1950s and was his assistant in New York in the 1960s. In 1998, Bill Parcells was the

Rex Ryan inspects his defense during a 2010 game.

head coach. The Jets gave Parcells the power to make all decisions about the roster, and he rewarded them with a trip to the AFC Championship Game.

Rex Ryan led the Jets to the conference title game in 2009 and 2010. Both times New York shocked the football experts. Ryan got his players to believe they could beat anyone—and they nearly proved him right. He showed that a coach's job is more than calling plays and running practices. Ryan reminded the Jets that playing football is hard work, but it can also be fun.

One Great Day

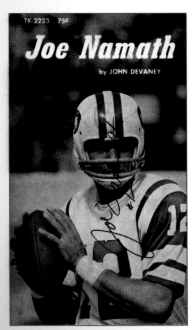

Growing up in Beaver Falls, Pennsylvania, Joe Namath idolized quarterback Johnny Unitas of the Baltimore Colts. Namath loved the way Unitas relied on his strong arm and sharp mind to win games. It was no accident that Namath ended up being the same kind of quarterback. But that was about all they had in common. Unitas had a flat-top crewcut, dressed plainly, and kept his thoughts to himself. Namath had long hair, wore wild clothes, and dated movie stars.

When the two stars met on the field, it was all about winning. In the second week of the 1972 season, the Jets traveled to Baltimore to face the Colts. Unitas was in his final year with his team. Namath had missed most of the 1971 season with an injury. Fans of both teams were hoping for the best. What they saw was the most unbelievable showcase of passing in NFL history.

LEFT: Joe Namath signed this copy of his biography.
RIGHT: Rich Caster

Namath and Unitas were in top form. They drilled pass after pass to their receivers, marching their teams up and down the field. The Colts played a **zone defense** in the first half, and Namath picked it apart. They played man-on-man in the second half, and Namath was even better.

The Jets held a slim lead in the fourth quarter when Namath saw Rich Caster running in the clear. He lofted a long pass that Caster ran down for a 79-yard touchdown. The next time New York had the ball, Caster faked the same play, changed direction, and broke free again. Namath hit him with an 80-yard scoring pass!

The Jets didn't have any better luck trying to defend Unitas. The 39-year-old legend rolled up 376 yards and three touchdowns. Namath, meanwhile, finished with 496 yards and six touchdowns. The Jets won, 44–34.

Legend Has It

Which Jet got the most out of his time playing in New York?

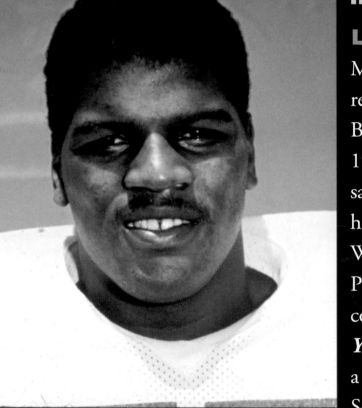

LEGEND HAS IT that Marvin Powell did. Powell represented the Jets in the Pro Bowl five times during the 1970s and 1980s. But some say the offensive lineman did his best work off the field. While playing for the Jets, Powell wrote a newspaper column, worked on the *New York Stock Exchange*, earned a degree from New York Law School, and served as the President of the NFL **Players Union**. Some fans wonder how he had time to play football!

ABOVE: Marvin Powell

Who was the best dancer on the Jets?

LEGEND HAS IT that Mark Gastineau was. Gastineau was one of the best pass-rushers in the NFL. Nothing gave him a bigger thrill than tackling the quarterback behind the **line of scrimmage**. After taking down an opposing passer, Gastineau would break into a wild "sack dance." Jets fans loved it, but the league had a different opinion. After the 1983 season—when Gastineau had 19 sacks and did his dance 19 times—the NFL passed a rule against "unsportsmanlike taunting."

Was the "Heidi Game" the Jets' most famous defeat?

LEGEND HAS IT that it was. In November of 1968, the Jets flew across the country to play the Oakland Raiders. Because the game was played on the West Coast, it was late on the East Coast by the time the fourth quarter began. The Jets were leading 32–29 with just over a minute left when suddenly the game blinked off the air. It was replaced by the TV movie *Heidi*. Jets fans were outraged—no one could believe the network stopped the coverage. They were even more angry when they learned the Raiders scored 14 points to win 43–32.

It Really Happened

n today's NFL, the one game that fans don't want to miss each week is played on Sunday night. But for many years, the league's most popular game was scheduled for Monday night. In fact, *Monday Night Football* was an American **tradition**. Millions of fans from all over the country stayed up late to see how the game turned out.

But that wasn't the case when the Jets met the Miami Dolphins on October 23, 2000. After three quarters, Miami was ahead 30–7. "This game is over," one of the Jets' own announcers said.

Not so fast. The Jets came alive and caught the Dolphins by surprise. Vinny Testaverde threw long touchdown passes to Laveranues Coles and Wayne Chrebet. The Jets scored another touchdown on a short pass, and

LEFT: Jumbo Elliott strains to control the ball before he hits the ground.
RIGHT: John Hall and holder Tom Tupa raise their arms in victory.

John Hall booted a field goal. New York tied the score 30–30!

The Dolphins recovered to take a 37–30 lead. But in the final moments, the Jets scored again on a trick play. Offensive lineman Jumbo Elliott batted, bobbled, and finally caught a pass in the end zone to send the game into overtime. Hall kicked a field goal a few minutes later to give the Jets a 40–37 victory.

New York's comeback was the greatest in the history of *Monday Night Football*—and the second-greatest ever in a game in the regular season. In the amazing fourth quarter, the Jets made 20 first downs, and of their four touchdowns, three were scored by players who had never reached the end zone before. To this day, Jets fans call the game the "Midnight Miracle."

Team Spirit

When you go to a Jets game, there is one cheer you can expect to hear again and again, "J-E-T-S! Jets! Jets! Jets!" It was originated by a pair of police officers who were big fans of Gang Green. But another fan named Ed Anzalone made the cheer a tradition. "Fireman Ed" leads the crowd in the chant during home games.

Jets fans are some of the most passionate fans in the NFL. Their mood during the week often depends on what happens on Sunday. When the Jets are winning, the fans can't stop bragging about them. When the team is losing, the players and coaches will hear about it.

Supporting the team is a family affair. Young fans learn to cheer for the Jets from their parents, grandparents, aunts, and uncles— some of whom started out rooting for the Titans more than 50 years ago.

LEFT: Ed Anzalone gets fired up.
ABOVE: This button was sold at the Polo Grounds during the early 1960s.

Timeline

In this timeline, each Super Bowl is listed under the year it was played. Remember that the Super Bowl is held early in the year and is actually part of the previous season. For example, Super Bowl XLVI was played on February 5, 2012, but it was the championship of the 2011 NFL season.

1960
The team plays its first season as the Titans.

1982
Freeman McNeil is the NFL's top rusher.

1965
Don Maynard ties for the AFL lead in touchdowns.

1969
The Jets win Super Bowl III.

1978
Wesley Walker leads the NFL in receiving yards.

Emerson Boozer helped the Jets win Super Bowl III.

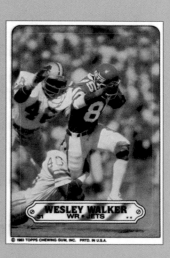

Wesley Walker

Curtis
Martin

Tim
Tebow

1998
Vinny Testaverde leads the Jets to a 12–4 record.

2004
Curtis Martin leads the NFL with 1,697 rushing yards.

2012
The Jets trade for Tim Tebow.

1988
Al Toon leads the NFL with 93 catches.

2011
Darrell Revis is named **All-Pro** for the third time.

Al
Toon

Fun Facts

MANY HAPPY RETURNS

In a 2011 game against the Denver Broncos, Darrelle Revis **intercepted** a pass at the goal line and returned it 100 yards for a touchdown. That tied a team record set by Aaron Glenn in 1996.

LET IT ROLL

In 1968, punter Steve O'Neill punted a ball from his own end zone against the Denver Broncos. The ball soared more than 70 yards in the air and rolled all the way to the other end of the field. It stopped just short of the goal line for a record 98-yard punt!

BIG SIX

In 2010, the Jets created their own Hall of Fame and called it the Ring of Honor. The first six people honored by the team were Weeb Ewbank, Winston Hill, Joe Klecko, Curtis Martin, Don Maynard, and Joe Namath.

RISE AND WALK

Dennis Byrd was a rising star with the Jets when he injured his neck and was *paralyzed* during a 1992 game. Doctors said he might never walk again. But Byrd made a miraculous recovery. Today he gives speeches to inspire other injury victims.

ROAD WARRIOR

In 2010, Mark Sanchez became only the second rookie in NFL history to win his first two playoff games. In both games, the Jets won despite being the visiting team.

A LITTLE ENGLISH

In 1972, Bobby Howfield led the AFC in scoring with 121 points. The 5′ 8″ kicker was an English soccer star who had never played a down of football before coming to the NFL. Howfield once scored four goals in a soccer game.

LEFT: Darrelle Revis
ABOVE: Dennis Byrd

Talking Football

"I truly believe that Wayne is the most beloved Jet ever to put on the uniform."
▶ **Marty Lyons**, *on Wayne Chrebet*

"He had a tremendous impact on a lot of people's lives, the way he conducted himself, the example he set, the way he tried to get the best out of you."
▶ **Matt Snell**, *on Weeb Ewbank*

"It's rotten when you lose, absolutely rotten. But there's one way to fix it and that's to win. And when you win, everything is great. So that's what we're planning on doing."
▶ **Rex Ryan**, *on winning and losing in the NFL*

"He's got such a great personality. I was like, 'Man, this is a really cool dude.' We clicked even before we knew we were going to be drafted together."

▶ **D'Brickashaw Ferguson,** *on Nick Mangold*

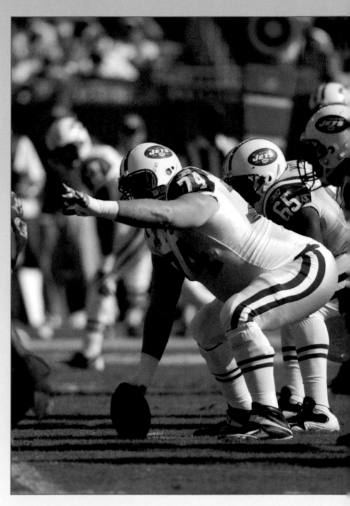

"When you have confidence, you can have a lot of fun. And when you have fun, you can do amazing things."

▶ **Joe Namath,** *on the joy of playing winning football*

"I value this job. It's my life."

▶ **Mark Sanchez,** *on being New York's starting quarterback*

"I always go until I can't go anymore."

▶ **Curtis Martin,** *on giving 100 percent every game*

LEFT: Marty Lyons
ABOVE: Nick Mangold

Great Debates

People who root for the Jets love to compare their favorite moments, teams, and players. Some debates have been going on for years! How would you settle these classic football arguments?

Curtis Martin was the Jets' greatest runner ...

... because he topped 1,000 yards season after season. In fact, he rushed for more than 1,000 yards seven years in a row for New York. Martin wasn't flashy like other stars. He just got the job done. Martin ran for more than 10,000 yards as a Jet and led the NFL in rushing yards in 2004. He also caught 367 passes and scored a total of 63 touchdowns.

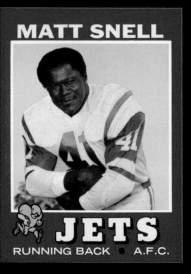

MATT SNELL
JETS
RUNNING BACK • A.F.C.

Not even close. If you needed to win one game, Matt Snell would be a no-brainer ...

... because he proved himself in the biggest game of all, the Super Bowl. Snell (   ) carried the ball 30 times and gained 121 yards in Super Bowl III. Thanks to him, Joe Namath didn't have to throw a single pass in the fourth quarter. Namath owed more than that to Snell—it was his powerful running during the 1960s that helped "Broadway Joe" become pro football's top passer.

Mark Gastineau was the team's most amazing defensive player ....

... because he used his size, speed, and power to change the way pass-rushers play the game. Gastineau (   ) was almost unstoppable. In 1984, he set a record with 22 sacks and added four more in the **Pro Bowl**. Gastineau was honored as an All-Pro every year from 1981 to 1985 and still holds the team's career mark for sacks.

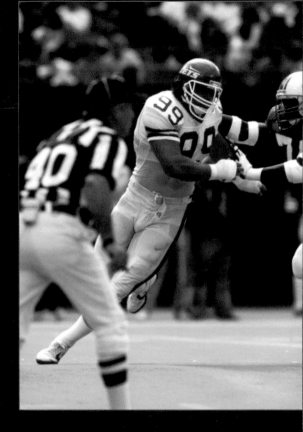

Really? Darrelle Revis is the definition of amazing ....

... because most teams totally gave up trying to throw passes in his direction. Revis played his best against the NFL's top receivers. In the Pro Bowl after the 2008 season, he brought fans to their feet with a one-handed interception. One year later, his diving interception against the San Diego Chargers in the playoffs turned the game around and helped the Jets reach the AFC Championship Game. How good was Revis? He was named All-Pro in 2010 even though he didn't intercept a single pass. That is one of the most amazing statistics in NFL history.

For the Record

The great Jets teams and players have left their marks on the record books. These are the "best of the best" …

Joe Namath

Chad Pennington

JETS AWARD WINNERS

WINNER	AWARD	YEAR
Matt Snell	AFL Rookie of the Year	1964
Joe Namath	AFL Rookie of the Year	1965
Joe Namath	AFL All-Star Game co-MVP	1966
Verlon Biggs	AFL All-Star Game co-MVP	1967
Don Maynard	AFL All-Star Game co-MVP	1968
Joe Namath	AFL All-Star Game co-MVP	1968
Joe Namath	AFL Most Valuable Player	1968
Joe Namath	Super Bowl III MVP	1969
Joe Namath	NFL Comeback Player of the Year	1974
Erik McMillan	NFL Defensive Rookie of the Year	1988
Hugh Douglas	NFL Defensive Rookie of the Year	1995
Jonathan Vilma	NFL Defensive Rookie of the Year	2004
Chad Pennington	NFL Comeback Player of the Year	2006

JETS ACHIEVEMENTS

ACHIEVEMENT	YEAR
AFL East Champions	1968
AFL Champions	1968
Super Bowl III Champions	1968*
AFL East Champions	1969
AFC East Champions	1998
AFC East Champions	2002

Super Bowls are played early the following year, but the game is counted as the championship of this season.

NEW YORK

WINSTON HILL   tackle-center

ABOVE: Winston Hill was the star of New York's offensive line in the 1960s.
LEFT: Bill Parcells led the Jets to the top of the AFC East in 1998.

Pinpoints

The history of a football team is made up of many smaller stories. These stories take place all over the map—not just in the city a team calls "home." Match the pushpins on these maps to the **Team Facts**, and you will begin to see the story of the Jets unfold!

TEAM FACTS

1 East Rutherford, New Jersey—*The Jets have played here since 1984.*

2 Beaver Falls, Pennsylvania—*Joe Namath was born here.*

3 Queens, New York—*The Jets won the 1968 AFL championship here.*

4 Richmond, Indiana—*Weeb Ewbank was born here.*

5 Knoxville, Tennessee—*Chad Pennington was born here.*

6 Miami, Florida—*The Jets won Super Bowl III here.*

7 Jackson, Mississippi—*Freeman McNeil was born here.*

8 Mobile, Alabama—*Rich Caster was born here.*

9 Armore, Oklahoma—*Mark Gastineau was born here.*

10 Martinez, California—*Jim Turner was born here.*

11 Makati City, Philippines—*Tim Tebow was born here.*

12 Bushey, England—*Bobby Howfield was born here.*

Jim Turner

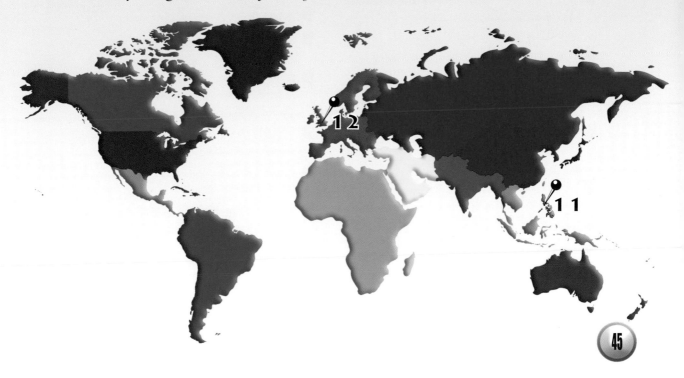

Glossary

AFC CHAMPIONSHIP GAME—The game played to determine which AFC team will go to the Super Bowl.

ALL-PRO—An honor given to the best players at their positions at the end of each season.

ALL-STAR—A player voted the best at his position.

AMERICAN FOOTBALL CONFERENCE (AFC)—One of two groups of teams that make up the NFL.

AMERICAN FOOTBALL LEAGUE (AFL)—The football league that began play in 1960 and later merged with the NFL.

ASSET—Something of value.

BACKFIELD—The players on offense who line up in back of the line of scrimmage.

DRAFTED—Chosen from a group of the best college players. The NFL draft is held each spring.

ERA—A period of time in history.

FIELD GOALS—Goals from the field, kicked over the crossbar and between the goal posts. A field goal is worth three points.

HALL OF FAME—The museum in Canton, Ohio, where football's greatest players are honored.

INTERCEPTED—Caught in the air by a defensive player.

LINE OF SCRIMMAGE—The imaginary line that separates the offense and defense before each play begins.

LOGO—A symbol or design that represents a company or team.

MERGED—Joined forces.

MOST VALUABLE PLAYER (MVP)—The award given each year to the league's best player; also given to the best player in the Super Bowl and Pro Bowl.

NATIONAL FOOTBALL LEAGUE (NFL)—The league that started in 1920 and is still operating today.

NEW YORK STOCK EXCHANGE—The place in New York City where people buy and sell shares of different companies.

PARALYZED—Unable to move a section of the body.

PLAYERS UNION—The organization that looks after the well-being of NFL players.

PLAYOFFS—The games played after the regular season to determine which teams play in the Super Bowl.

PRO BOWL—The NFL's all-star game, played after the regular season.

PROFESSIONAL—Paid to play.

REMARKABLE—Unusual or exceptional.

REPUTATION—A belief or opinion about someone.

ROOKIE—A player in his first season.

SACK—A tackle of the quarterback behind the line of scrimmage.

SUPER BOWL—The championship of the NFL, played between the winners of the National Football Conference and American Football Conference.

TRADITION—A belief or custom that is handed down from generation to generation.

UNDERDOGS—A group of people not expected to achieve a goal or succeed.

ZONE DEFENSE—A defense in which players are responsible for guarding an area of the field rather than covering a specific offensive player.

OVERTIME

TEAM SPIRIT introduces a great way to stay up to date with your team! Visit our **OVERTIME** link and get connected to the latest and greatest updates. **OVERTIME** serves as a young reader's ticket to an exclusive web page—with more stories, fun facts, team records, and photos of the Jets. Content is updated during and after each season. The **OVERTIME** feature also enables readers to send comments and letters to the author!

Log onto:

www.norwoodhousepress.com/library.aspx

and click on the tab: **TEAM SPIRIT** to access **OVERTIME**.

Read all the books in the series to learn more about professional sports. For a complete listing of the baseball, basketball, football, and hockey teams in the **TEAM SPIRIT** series, visit our website at:

www.norwoodhousepress.com/library.aspx

On the Road

NEW YORK JETS
20 Murray Hill Parkway
East Rutherford, New Jersey 07073
973-549-4800
www.newyorkjets.com

THE PRO FOOTBALL HALL OF FAME
2121 George Halas Drive NW
Canton, Ohio 44708
330-456-8207
www.profootballhof.com

On the Bookshelf

To learn more about the sport of football, look for these books at your library or bookstore:

- Frederick, Shane. *The Best of Everything Football Book.* North Mankato, Minnesota: Capstone Press, 2011.

- Jacobs, Greg. *The Everything Kids' Football Book: The All-Time Greats, Legendary Teams, Today's Superstars—And Tips on Playing Like a Pro.* Avon, Massachusetts: Adams Media Corporation, 2010.

- Editors of *Sports Illustrated for Kids. 1st and 10: Top 10 Lists of Everything in Football.* New York, New York: Sports Illustrated Books, 2011.

Index

PAGE NUMBERS IN **BOLD** REFER TO ILLUSTRATIONS.

About the Author

MARK STEWART has written more than 50 books on football and over 150 sports books for kids. He grew up in New York City during the 1960s rooting for the Giants and Jets, and was lucky enough to meet players from both teams. Mark comes from a family of writers. His grandfather was Sunday Editor of *The New York Times,* and his mother was Articles Editor of *Ladies' Home Journal* and *McCall's*. Mark has profiled hundreds of athletes over the past 25 years. He has also written several books about his native New York and New Jersey, his home today. Mark is a graduate of Duke University, with a degree in history. He lives and works in a home overlooking Sandy Hook, New Jersey. You can contact Mark through the Norwood House Press website.